Asombrosos anima

T0014332

MARIPOSAS

Bray Jacobson
Traducido por Diana Osorio

Gareth Stevens
PUBLISHING

Please visit our website, www.garethstevens.com. For a free color catalog of all our high-quality books, call toll free 1-800-542-2595 or fax 1-877-542-2596.

Library of Congress Cataloging-in-Publication Data
Names: Jacobson, Bray, author.
Title: Mariposas / Bray Jacobson.
Description: New York : Gareth Stevens Publishing, [2022] | Series: Asombrosos animalitos | Includes index.
Identifiers: LCCN 2020006215 | ISBN 9781538269138 (paperback) | ISBN 9781538269145 (6 Pack)| ISBN 9781538269152 (library binding) | ISBN 9781538269169 (ebook)
Subjects: LCSH: Butterflies–Juvenile literature.
Classification: LCC QL544.2 .J34 2022 | DDC 595.78/9–dc23
LC record available at https://lccn.loc.gov/2020006215

First Edition

Published in 2022 by
Gareth Stevens Publishing
111 East 14th Street, Suite 349
New York, NY 10003

Copyright © 2022 Gareth Stevens Publishing

Translator: Diana Osorio
Editor, Spanish: Rossana Zúñiga
Designer: Katelyn E. Reynolds

Photo credits: Cover, p. 1 YURI CORTEZ/AFP via Getty Images; pp. 5, 23 borchee/E+/Getty Images; pp. 7, 24 (wings) Garry Gay/ Photographer's Choice / Getty Images Plus; p. 9 Kelly Kalhoefer/The Image Bank / Getty Images Plus; p. 11 Louise Docker Sydney Australia/Moment/Getty Images; p. 13 Robert Landau/ Corbis Documentary/Getty Images; pp. 15, 24 (eggs) Wild Horizon/Universal Images Group via Getty Images; p. 17 teptong/ iStock / Getty Images Plus; pp. 19, 24 (pupa) stanley45/E+/Getty Images; p. 21 Willowpix/E+/ Getty Images.

Printed in the United States of America

Some of the images in this book illustrate individuals who are models. The depictions do not imply actual situations or events.

CPSIA compliance information: Batch #CSGS22: For further information contact Gareth Stevens, New York, New York at 1-800-542-2595.

Find us on

Contenido

¡Las mariposas son activas!
Salen en el día.

La mayoría tiene
dos pares de alas.

Tienen seis patas.

Comen plantas.
Beben de las flores.

Pueden volar distancias largas.

Las mariposas
ponen huevos.

Los bebés
parecen gusanos.

Descansan como pupas.
Sus cuerpos cambian.

¡Se convierten
en mariposas!

Son de
colores brillantes.

Palabras que debes aprender

huevos

pupa

alas

Índice